T0053758

Living God's Dream
Dismantling Racism for Children

Participant Guide

Sally Ulrey, Katie McRee, and Malinda Shamburger

The Diocese of Atlanta
In collaboration with the Absalom Jones Center for Racial Healing

Church
PUBLISHING

Copyright ©2024 the Diocese of Atlanta and Sally Ulrey, Katie McRee, and Malinda Shamburger

All rights reserved. Except for pages that are marked with permission to reproduce, no part of this book may be reproduced in any form without permission in writing from the publisher.

All scripture quotations, unless otherwise indicated, are taken from the Holy Bible New International Version®. Copyright © 1973, 1978, 1984 International Bible Society. Used by permission of Zondervan Publishing House. All rights reserved. The "NIV" and "New International Version" trademarks are registered in the United States Patent and Trademark Office by International Bible Society. Use of either trademark requires permission of International Bible Society.

Scripture quotations marked (NRSV) are from the New Revised Standard Version Bible, copyright © 1989 National Council of the Churches of Christ in the United States of America. Used by permission. All rights reserved worldwide.

The Episcopal Diocese of Atlanta www.episcopalatlanta.org
The Absalom Jones Center for Racial Healing
www.centerforracialhealing.org

Church Publishing
19 East 34th Street
New York, NY 10016
www.churchpublishing.org

Typesetting by Nord Compo
Cover design by: Ink Splatter Design

ISBN: 978-1-64065-681-9
eISBN: 978-1-64065-680-2

Library of Congress Control Number: 2024930701

I Am Beloved

We are all pieces of the puzzle, and we need every piece!

Label the puzzle pieces with the names of those around you. Without everyone, something would be missing!

I Am Beloved

Scripture Story

So God created humankind in his image, in the image of God he created them; male and female he created them. God blessed them…
—Genesis 1:27–28

After this I looked, and there was a great multitude that no one could count, from every nation, from all tribes and peoples and languages, standing before the throne and before the Lamb, robed in white, with palm branches in their hands.
—Rev. 7:9

I Am Beloved

Scripture Story

God's Dream is that everyone love God and love each other, and that we would see the beauty of God in each person God created, that we would live in harmony with God's creation and all of the people God created.

Draw a picture of what it would look like if God's Dream (loving God and each other, living in harmony) came to life.

What was my favorite part of the story?

What can I do today to help God's dream come to life?

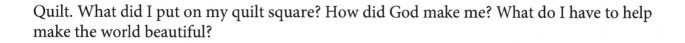

Art

Quilt. What did I put on my quilt square? How did God make me? What do I have to help make the world beautiful?

What did those around me put on their quilt squares? What do I like about how God created them?

We need each other to see the beauty of God more fully, and together we make a beautiful quilt!

I Am Beloved

Activity

12 Just as a body, though one, has many parts, but all its many parts form one body, so it is with Christ. 13 For we were all baptized by one Spirit so as to form one body—whether Jews or Gentiles, slave or free—and we were all given the one Spirit to drink. 14 Even so the body is not made up of one part but of many.
—1 Corinthians 12

Everyone is good at something! We need each other! In your group:

Who is like a "brain" and gives good directions?

Who is like the "eyes" and sees things others don't notice?

Who is like a "mouth" and can express themselves clearly and tell people what the situation needs?

Who is like the "hands" and likes to serve and be helpers?

Who is like the "feet" and likes to move toward others to help them?

Who is like the "heart" and loves everyone and shows them kindness?

I Am Beloved

Activity (pg 1)

We need every part of the Body!

Cut the body parts out and glue them on the Body

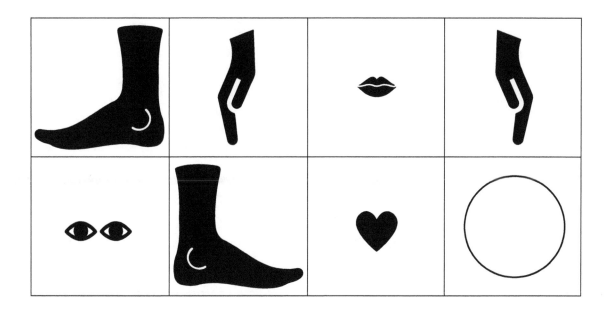

I Am Beloved

Activity (pg 2)

I Am Beloved

Serve

Circle the gifts God gave me.

Creative
Steadfast/Dependable
Loving
Beautiful
Merciful
Wise
Patient
Strong
Generous
Kind
Fair
Gentle

When I use these gifts, I show others what God is like!!

What is one way I use my favorite gift or quality? (Example: If my favorite quality is creative, how do I show that? Building things? Drawing pictures?)

List some ways I see God's goodness in other people in this room. Put their name and something good I see in them.

I Am Beloved

Summary Sheet

- Every human being is made in God's image, which means each person has something good, and that goodness shows us something about what God is like.
- Racial differences in human beings are intended by God, and they are beautiful.
- Without all of humanity, we wouldn't see the whole picture of who God is.
- It is important to practice seeing the image of God in others.
- Everyone has gifts, and our differences teach us something about the world.
- We need each other and the different gifts we all bring to the table

Together we make a beautiful picture

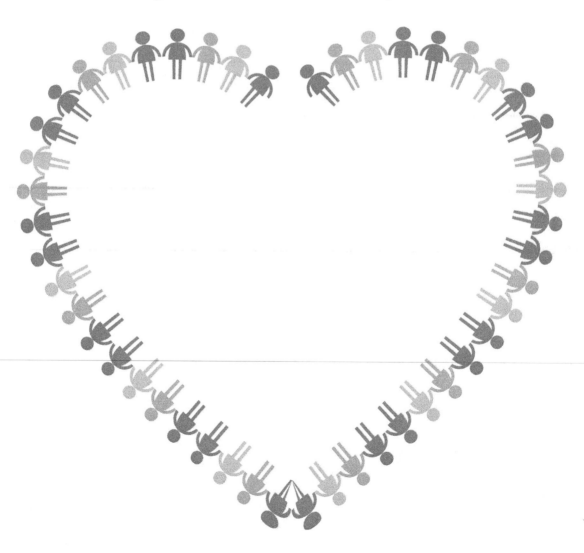

I Am Brave

Describe a time when I made a mess. How did that feel?

What did I do to clean up the mess or make it right or put things back together?

What have I learned for the next time that I see a mess about how to help?

I Am Brave

Scripture Story

[3] *Now Israel loved Joseph more than any of his other sons, because he had been born to him in his old age; and he made an ornate robe for him.* [4] *When his brothers saw that their father loved him more than any of them, they hated him and could not speak a kind word to him....*

[14] *So [Jacob] said to [Joseph], "Go and see if all is well with your brothers and with the flocks, and bring word back to me."*

[17b] *So Joseph went after his brothers and found them near Dothan.* [18] *But they saw him in the distance, and before he reached them, they plotted to kill him.*

[19] *"Here comes that dreamer!" they said to each other.* [20] *"Come now, let's kill him and throw him into one of these cisterns and say that a ferocious animal devoured him. Then we'll see what comes of his dreams."*

[21] *When Reuben heard this, he tried to rescue him from their hands. "Let's not take his life," he said.* [22] *"Don't shed any blood. Throw him into this cistern here in the wilderness, but don't lay a hand on him." Reuben said this to rescue him from them and take him back to his father.*

[26] *Judah said to his brothers, "What will we gain if we kill our brother and cover up his blood?* [27] *Come, let's sell him to the Ishmaelites and not lay our hands on him; after all, he is our brother, our own flesh and blood." His brothers agreed.*

[28] *So when the Midianite merchants came by, his brothers pulled Joseph up out of the cistern and sold him for twenty shekels of silver to the Ishmaelites, who took him to Egypt.*
—Genesis 37 (Excerpts). The story continues in Genesis chapters 41-45.

I Am Brave

Scripture Story

Write about it or draw a picture of each part of the story, and show what each person might have been feeling.

Joseph, with his fancy coat which meant he was his father's favorite, bragging to his brothers about his dreams of how they would bow down to him.	Joseph in the well; Reuben trying to stop the brothers from killing him.
Joseph, in charge of everything in Egypt, when he recognized his brothers, who were bowing down to him, trying to buy grain.	Joseph and his brothers, when Joseph reveals who he is.

I Am Brave

Scripture Story

[4] *Then Joseph said to his brothers, "Come close to me." When they had done so, he said, "I am your brother Joseph, the one you sold into Egypt!* [5] *And now, do not be distressed and do not be angry with yourselves for selling me here, because it was to save lives that God sent me ahead of you."*

[15] *And he kissed all his brothers and wept over them. Afterward his brothers talked with him.*
—Genesis 45

Joseph and his brothers start to try to repair the mess they've made of their relationship.

I Am Brave

Scripture Story

Joseph and his brothers got into a fight. Sometimes, we need to be like Joseph's brothers and make right the wrongs we've done. Sometimes, we need to be like Joseph and forgive those who have wronged us when they are working to make it right.

Write or draw about a time when someone wronged me.

Write or draw about a time when I wronged someone else.

Write or draw about how people can put things right after wrong has been done.

I Am Brave

Story Book

What was my favorite part of the story?

How was the person in the story brave?

What ideas does this give ME about how to be brave in my life? Is there a situation where I need courage?

I Am Brave

Art

When we are brave, and face our mistakes, God can make something beautiful out of it!

Describe the beautiful art project I made out of the broken pieces.

Is there anything in my life that feels broken or not quite the way it's supposed to be? Say a prayer and ask God to help make something beautiful out of it.

Who do I need to help you or who do I need to talk to about this?

Draw picture of something beautiful.

I Am Brave

Activity

What activity did I do?

What were some things I have done to demonstrate bravery? How did it feel to think about those things?

What are some ways I want to demonstrate bravery today, tomorrow, or this week?

I Am Brave

Serve

Ways to Be Brave!

1. Apologize to someone you have hurt. Ask if there is anything you can do to make it better.

2. Watch for people who need help. It may be a family member or someone you encounter while you are out with your family. Be brave and help them!

3. Is there a child at school, on the playground, or at one of your activities that is being left out? Invite them specifically to join you.

4. If you hear anyone speaking unkindly about another person, stop them. Tell them that you are not okay with what they are saying. If they won't stop, move away from them and do not participate in the conversation.

5. Do you know of anyone that is struggling? Think about all the people you know: your family, friends, teachers, coaches, neighbors, church family, etc. It can include adults! Make them a card or other small treat to offer encouragement.

6. Keep a look out for the ways that those around you are special. Pay them a compliment and let them know how they are special.

7. Read about advocacy groups, like the Native American Healing Coalition, that are working to clean up some of the messes in the world. Think about how they might inspire you to do some work of your own.

Which one of these do I want to try?

Once I've done one of these, I'll record here how it went and how I felt as I did it:

I Am Brave

Summary Sheet

- God's Dream: Differences are intended by God and are beautiful.
- The mess: Humans have often responded to differences with unkindness and unfairness. We make a mess of our relationships.
- Being Brave: When we see that differences have separated us, we must be brave to reach out and invite others to come together as God intended. When we see that there is a mess (hurt, people being left out, unfairness), we must be brave to face the messes and try to work on them and fix them.
- With God's help, we can help make the messes into something beautiful.

Help put the world back together

I Am Compassionate

When God looks at me, what do I imagine God sees that I don't see? How do I look to God? Draw a picture of myself the way God sees me (with extra love!)

I Am Compassionate

Scripture Story

But Ruth replied, "Don't urge me to leave you or to turn back from you. Where you go I will go, and where you stay I will stay. Your people will be my people and your God my God. [17] Where you die I will die, and there I will be buried. May the Lord deal with me, be it ever so severely, if even death separates you and me." [18] When Naomi realized that Ruth was determined to go with her, she stopped urging her.

[11] Boaz replied, "I've been told all about what you have done for your mother-in-law since the death of your husband—how you left your father and mother and your homeland and came to live with a people you did not know before. [12] May the Lord repay you for what you have done. May you be richly rewarded by the Lord, the God of Israel, under whose wings you have come to take refuge."
—Ruth, especially 1:16—18, 2:11—12

I Am Compassionate

Scripture Story

Compassion is coming alongside someone who is suffering or struggling like a friend, trying to understand, and trying to help.

When God looked at Ruth and Naomi, what do I imagine God saw? Draw Naomi and Ruth with my God glasses on…how God sees them with compassion and love.

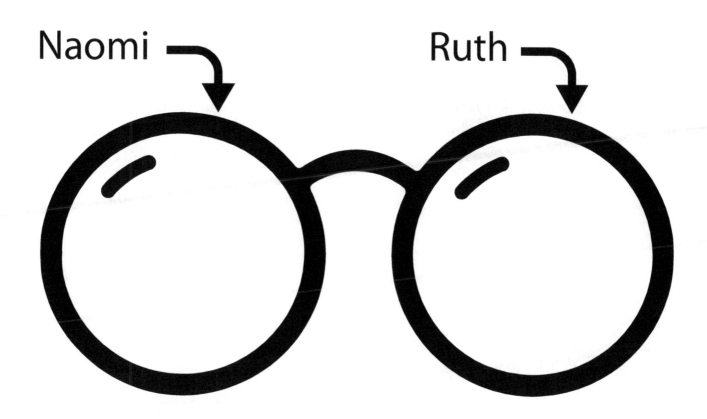

I Am Compassionate

Story Book

What was my favorite part?

Compassion is coming alongside someone like a friend, trying to understand, and trying to help. Who in the story tried to help?

How can I try to help someone else today or this week?

I Am Compassionate

Art: "Hearts of Compassion"

Left side: How I've seen people struggle. Right side: Ideas on how I can help.

I Am Compassionate

Activity

What was my favorite part of the activities I did?

When did I feel good during the activities? What was a "high?"

When did I feel not-so-good during the activities? Describe any "lows."

How can I show compassion and include people next time someone is left out?

I Am Compassionate

Serve

What was it like to make meals for someone else who needs one, maybe someone I've never even met?

Write or draw a prayer for the person or people who receive the meals you made. What do you hope for them?

I Am Compassionate

Summary Sheet

- Compassion is coming alongside someone who is suffering or struggling like a friend, trying to understand, and trying to help.
- God is compassionate. God comes alongside us, tries to understand, and helps us.
- We need to look at others through God's eyes of compassion.

SEE OTHERS THROUGH GOD GLASSES

I Am Resistant

Have I ever felt pressured to go along with something I didn't feel was right? What happened?

Have I ever resisted going along with something I didn't feel was right? What happened?

I Am Resistant

Scripture Story #1 – Choosing the Right Food

In the third year of the reign of Jehoiakim king of Judah, Nebuchadnezzar king of Babylon came to Jerusalem and besieged it. ²And the Lord delivered Jehoiakim king of Judah into his hand, along with some of the articles from the temple of God. These he carried off to the temple of his god in Babylonia and put in the treasure house of his god.

³Then the king ordered Ashpenaz, chief of his court officials, to bring into the king's service some of the Israelites from the royal family and the nobility...

⁶Among those who were chosen were some from Judah: Daniel, Hananiah, Mishael and Azariah. ⁷The chief official gave them new names: to Daniel, the name Belteshazzar; to Hananiah, Shadrach; to Mishael, Meshach; and to Azariah, Abednego.

⁸But Daniel resolved not to defile himself with the royal food and wine, and he asked the chief official for permission not to defile himself this way. ⁹Now God had caused the official to show favor and compassion to Daniel, ¹⁰but the official told Daniel, "I am afraid of my lord the king, who has assigned your food and drink. Why should he see you looking worse than the other young men your age? The king would then have my head because of you."

¹¹Daniel then said to the guard whom the chief official had appointed over Daniel, Hananiah, Mishael and Azariah, ¹²"Please test your servants for ten days: Give us nothing but vegetables to eat and water to drink. ¹³Then compare our appearance with that of the young men who eat the royal food, and treat your servants in accordance with what you see." ¹⁴So he agreed to this and tested them for ten days.

¹⁵At the end of the ten days they looked healthier and better nourished than any of the young men who ate the royal food. ¹⁶So the guard took away their choice food and the wine they were to drink and gave them vegetables instead.
—Daniel 1

I Am Resistant

Scripture Story #1 – Choosing the Right Food

Daniel asked to eat vegetables

I Am Resistant

Scripture Story #2 – Prayer

³ *Now Daniel so distinguished himself among the administrators and the satraps by his exceptional qualities that the king planned to set him over the whole kingdom.* ⁴ *At this, the administrators and the satraps tried to find grounds for charges against Daniel in his conduct of government affairs, but they were unable to do so. They could find no corruption in him, because he was trustworthy and neither corrupt nor negligent.* ⁵ *Finally these men said, "We will never find any basis for charges against this man Daniel unless it has something to do with the law of his God."*

⁶ *So these administrators and satraps went as a group to the king and said: "May King Darius live forever!* ⁷ *The royal administrators, prefects, satraps, advisers and governors have all agreed that the king should issue an edict and enforce the decree that anyone who prays to any god or human being during the next thirty days, except to you, Your Majesty, shall be thrown into the lions' den.* ⁸ *Now, Your Majesty, issue the decree and put it in writing so that it cannot be altered—in accordance with the law of the Medes and Persians, which cannot be repealed."* ⁹ *So King Darius put the decree in writing.*

¹⁰ *Now when Daniel learned that the decree had been published, he went home to his upstairs room where the windows opened toward Jerusalem. Three times a day he got down on his knees and prayed, giving thanks to his God, just as he had done before….*

¹⁶ *So the king gave the order, and they brought Daniel and threw him into the lions' den. The king said to Daniel, "May your God, whom you serve continually, rescue you!"*

¹⁷ *A stone was brought and placed over the mouth of the den, and the king sealed it with his own signet ring and with the rings of his nobles, so that Daniel's situation might not be changed…*

¹⁹ *At the first light of dawn, the king got up and hurried to the lions' den.* ²⁰ *When he came near the den, he called to Daniel in an anguished voice, "Daniel, servant of the living God, has your God, whom you serve continually, been able to rescue you from the lions?"*

²¹ *Daniel answered, "May the king live forever!* ²² *My God sent his angel, and he shut the mouths of the lions. They have not hurt me, because I was found innocent in his sight. Nor have I ever done any wrong before you, Your Majesty."*
—Daniel 6

I Am Resistant

Scripture Story #2 – Prayer

I Am Resistant

Scripture Story

As I watched and played the stories about Daniel, what did I learn about resisting unfairness?

Did I play Daniel? The lions? Others? What was that like?

When have I seen someone being treated unfairly or worse than other people?

What can I do next time I see unfairness to resist it?

I Am Resistant

Story Book

What was my favorite part of the story?

How did I see someone in the story resisting (or not going along with) unfairness?

When have I witnessed someone being treated unfairly?

Next time I see someone being treated unfairly, what ideas do I have for resisting that (or not going along with it)?

I Am Resistant

Art

What thing did I want to protest against or change? What thing did I not want to go along with because it seems unfair or wrong?

What did I put on my sign?

What ideas do I have about working on this particular unfair thing? What else might I do?

Write or draw a prayer asking God to help me work on this.

I Am Resistant

Activity

What activities did I do? What did I notice about the keys to these activities?

What did I learn about resistance, or not going along with something, from these activities?

Next time I need to resist, or not go along with unfairness, in my life, what ideas do I have now?

Draw a picture of someone standing firm or resisting.

I Am Resistant

Serve

How did it feel to hold my sign and march around our space?

What did I learn from this activity that I don't want to forget. Record here.

I Am Resistant

Summary Sheet

- Resistance means to stand firm against something. It means not going along with unfairness.
- Resisting unfairness is a way to help the world become more fair and good, like God intended.

Resist Unfairness!!

I Am Ready

Trace your hand. List 5 different ways you use your hands to help people!

I Am Ready

Scripture Story

My brothers and sisters, believers in our glorious Lord Jesus Christ must not show favoritism. Suppose a man comes into your meeting wearing a gold ring and fine clothes, and a poor man in filthy old clothes also comes in. If you show special attention to the man wearing fine clothes and say, "Here's a good seat for you," but say to the poor man, "You stand there" or "Sit on the floor by my feet," have you not discriminated among yourselves and become judges with evil thoughts?

If you really keep the royal law found in Scripture, "Love your neighbor as yourself," you are doing right. But if you show favoritism, you sin and are convicted by the law as lawbreakers.

What good is it, my brothers and sisters, if someone claims to have faith but has no deeds? Can such faith save them? Suppose a brother or a sister is without clothes and daily food. If one of you says to them, "Go in peace; keep warm and well fed," but does nothing about their physical needs, what good is it? In the same way, faith by itself, if it is not accompanied by action, is dead.
—James 2:1—4, 8-9, 14—17

I Am Ready

Scripture Story

What did the Scripture say about "favoritism" (when people are not treated equally, but some people are treated better than others)?

What skits did I see about situations where people were treated unfairly? What skits did I do, and what part did I play? What did that feel like to watch or participate in the skit in that role?

What did I learn about how to handle those situations where someone was treated unfairly? What do I want to remember and record below so I don't forget!

I Am Ready

Story Book

What was my favorite part of the story?

How did the people in the story work on a problem in the world?

What problems do I want to work on in the world?

What are some ideas I have about how I can do what I can do to work on those problems?

Art

What artwork did I create today?

What does that piece of art mean to me? What does it help me remember?

What words or phrases from this quotation do I really like? Circle, underline, or decorate them.

Christ Has No Body
Christ has no body but yours,
No hands, no feet on earth but yours,
Yours are the eyes with which he looks
Compassion on this world,
Yours are the feet with which he walks to do good,
Yours are the hands, with which he blesses all the world.
Yours are the hands, yours are the feet,
Yours are the eyes, you are his body.
Christ has no body now but yours,
No hands, no feet on earth but yours,
Yours are the eyes with which he looks
compassion on this world.
Christ has no body now on earth but yours.
Teresa of Avila (1515–1582)

I Am Ready

Activity

The activity shows us that we need each other, and that we all need to work together, so that we can work on the problems in this world.

For the problems in this world that I want to fix, who do I know that can help me?

I Am Ready

Serve

Here are some ways my church or community is working on some of the problems in this world (My teacher may be able to tell me more about this.):

Here are some ways I can join them (My teacher may be able to tell me more about this.):

What do I need to tell my grown-ups about how this so that I can join my community in this work? (Record details, dates, times, locations about service opportunities below.).

I Am Ready

Summary Sheet

- We are the ones God has asked to do the work. It's up to us. God will help.
- We are ready to take action! We are loved. We are brave. We are compassionate. We can resist the ways the world doesn't do it right.
- We have feet to go to where the needs are. We have hands to serve. We have hearts to love. We can do it!

Printed in the USA
CPSIA information can be obtained
at www.ICGtesting.com
JSHW060233290324
60144JS00004B/10